BOOK-WORM DROPPINGS

An Anthology of Absurd Remarks
Made by Customers in Secondhand Bookshops

Collected by
Shaun Tyas

With illustrations by
Martin Smith

Published by: PAUL WATKINS
STAMFORD, 1988

Published in Great Britain by Paul Watkins,
45 St. Leonards's St., Stamford, Lincolnshire, PE9 2HN.

ISBN
Hardback: 1 871615 00 3
Softback: 1 871615 01 1

Photoset by Parker Typesetting Service, Leicester.
Printed and bound by Woolnoughs of Irthlingborough.

CONTENTS

ACKNOWLEDGEMENTS

Thanks are due to Barry Shaw, editor of *The Bookdealer*, for printing extracts from the collection over several weeks, thereby provoking many further contributions, and to all those fellow dealers who shared their experiences with me. Their names are listed below. The absence of contributions from some dealers perhaps reflects their own sense of humour (or lack of it) rather than the sanity of their customers!

I am very grateful to my friend Martin Smith for spending so much time drawing the lovely cartoons. Sometimes he appears to be utterly repellent, but most of the time he's all right.

Philip Riley very kindly proof-read my final version, and even re-read it after corrections were made.

The enthusiasm of the other staff of Goldmark Books and the two Galleries hardly need be mentioned, but I thought I would anyway: Catherine, Cynthia, Deirdre, Hilary, Judith, Rachel, Richard, Simon and Mike and Sue Goldmark without whom there would have been no bookshop and no book.

Jill and Colin Wright of Colin Wright Associates, Uppingham, and Albert Williams of Parker Typesetting Service, Leicester, gave advice on various computer problems.

Many other friends made helpful suggestions and helped with informal support, especially Angela and Alex of the Lord Burghley pub; Bob, Brian, Caroline, Christopher, Colin, Dave, Del, Ernie, Fran, Frizzle, Graham, Ishobel, Jane, Janet, Janice, John, Joyce, Kiran, Lloyd, Marc, Markos, Martin, Mitch, Nikki, Paul, Sara, Scottie and Simon *and everyone else*.

Further contributions, sent to the publisher, would be most welcome, especially from shops selling new books. If this one sells, we'll do another!

This book is dedicated to all those marvellous, larger-than-life characters who inspired it. There have been many who could not be recorded because their eccentricity did not manifest itself in any single absurd remark, but they all contributed to the general atmosphere of amusement.

CONTRIBUTORS

(Including those whose Droppings have not appeared)

BANBURY BOOKSHOP, Banbury; P.N. BARNARD, Maidenhead; BEN BASS, Marshfield; BATH BOOK EXCHANGE, Bath; BECK HEAD BOOKS, Kirkby Lonsdale; FRED BETTLEY, Richmond, North Yorkshire; BIRMINGHAM BOOKSHOP, Birmingham; BLAENAVON BOOKSHOP, Blaenavon; BLITZGEIST BOOKSHOP, Birmingham; THE BOOK NOOK, Fort William; BOOKS AND CHATTELS, Ludlow; BOOKS ETC., Stamford; THE BOOKSHOP, Belfast; THE BOOKSHOP, Blakeney; BORDER BOOKSHOP, Todmorden; ALAN BRETT, London; N.F. BROOKES, Brighton; THE CAVERN, Haslemere; CHAPEL COLLECTORS' CENTRE, Castor; CHEYNE LANE BOOKSHOP, Stamford; COLUMBINE BOOKS, Southampton; COUNTY BOOKSHOP, Oakham; J. and G. CURTIS, Hornsea; MRS. M.L. DAVIES, Sutton Coldfield; REBECCA DEARMAN, Leicester; NIAL DEVITT BOOKS, Leamington Spa; WILLIAM DINNER, Brighton; DOGGIE HUBBARD'S BOOKSHOP, Aberystwyth; DAVID FLINT, Basingstoke; STEPHEN FOSTER, Wandsworth; STEWART W. GIBBS, Largs; RICHARD GILBERTSON, Launceston; M. & R. GLENDALE, London; GOSFORD BOOKS, Coventry; GREEN MEADOW, Kinoulton; G. K. HADFIELD, Shepshed; TERRY HALE and MARTIN STONE, Paris, France; GRAHAM HODGE, Wellingborough; R.F.G. HOLLETT & SON, Sedbergh; PETER HOWARD (BOOKS), South Croydon; RICHARD HUMM, Stamford; DAVE JACKSON, Gloucester; IAN JACKSON, Berkeley, California; JERMY & WESTERMAN, Nottingham; JEROBY BOOKS, Oadby; DAVID JOHNSTONE, Eaton Ford; JUST BOOKS, Truro; JUST BOOKS, Uppingham; BEN KANE BOOK SERVICE, London; MRS. A. KENT, Framlingham; REG. LEET, Market Harborough; LEICESTER UNIVERSITY BOOKSHOP, Leicester; LOUIS LEOPOLD, March; LITTLE HOLCOMBE BOOKS, Ramsbottom; NORMAN LORD, London; LORIEN BOOKS, Kirkmichael; C.E.B. MAWSON, while at Foyles, London; LOUISE McDERMOTT, Rome, Italy; BRIAN MILLS, Newcastle-upon-Tyne; MOLE BOOKSHOP, East Molesey; MR. BADGER'S BOOKSHOP, Taunton; MR. MULLARNEY, Dublin; W. MUSGROVE, Plymouth; OBAN ANTIQUES, Oban; THE OBSERVATORY, Simka, Alaska; OCCULTIQUE, Northampton; OLD SOKE BOOKS, Peterborough; C.D. PARAMOR, Newmarket; PARKINGTON BOOKS, Billingham; D.M. PIERCY, Colchester; MARGARET POLE, Thaxted; POMES PENYEACH, Newcastle-under-Lyme; A.J. REDSTONE, Nottingham; RHOS POINT BOOKS, Rhos-on-Sea; ROOM AT THE TOP, Kingsbridge; THE RUTLAND BOOKSHOP, Uppingham; THE SCULPTURE STUDIO, Uppingham; PETER SKINNER, New York; IVY EARL SMITH, Torquay; KEN SPELMAN, York; SPCA CHARITY BOOKSHOP, Mosta, Malta; ANDREW STEWART, Helpringham; NORMAN T. STOREY, London; SUSAN TAYLOR, Honley; TITLES, Oxford; ROBERT VAUGHAN, Stratford-on-Avon; EUNICE WATKINS, Maidstone; RICHARD WAY, Henley-on-Thames; JACQUELINE WESLEY, London; CHRISTOPHER WILLIAMS, Poole; NICHOLAS WILLMOTT, Ipswich; WOODSTOCK BOOKSHOP, Woodstock; RUSSELL WRAGG, Leek; WYRD BOOK COMPANY, Saxmundham.

INTRODUCTION

The second-hand book trade is a way of life, and this collection of anecdotes is offered as a celebration of it. Its humour derives from both the general absurdity of the book world and from that other great source of amusement, the practice of buying and selling.

For a start, there is nothing quite like serving the public. Shopkeepers everywhere put up with a barrage of inane and trivial comments and requests all day long. We manage to make a living out of it, and usually keep our patience and our sanity, but we are entitled to redress the balance a little by having a laugh once the customer has gone.

They can be exasperatingly vague ("There's a book . . ."), or irritatingly specific (it *has* to be the 1985 Penguin edition, none other). They can take months to make a decision, but expect you to perform miracles immediately. They interrupt. They hover round you when you're pricing or sorting new stock. They ignore everything you say, and the more effusive their language, the less they are actually interested. If you appear prosperous, they expect a discount; if you appear to be in difficulties, they also expect a discount. They don't want to look for books themselves. They never have their cheque-books or their glasses with them and they move books from one shelf to another.

Dealers can be no less awkward than their customers. When we are bored with the lack of trade or driven to distraction by the financial or personal demands of our calling, we are not above taking it out on the first fellow-dealer to walk through the door, or the next person who calls trying to sell books of minimal financial interest. It's something to do with being a human being.

There is much diversity in the world of books. On the one hand the trade has the appearance of gentle scholarship, on the other it is extremely earthy. I have chosen to celebrate the coarser aspects of the trade because it seems to me that the average second-hand bookdealer lives in chaos. The customers seem to prefer it that way, rather than be excluded when we need to 'tidy up'. Order is intimidating after all. Some observers think that the trade is staffed by inadequates and drop-outs, but they don't realise how much thought goes into that carefully-nurtured Dickensian image.

The book trade has everything. There is the pleasure of dealing with beautiful and interesting items, but this is combined with the cut-and-thrust of the market place and even with physical exercise. Books will keep you fit if they are heavy enough. It is marvellous fun to buy books and to earn a living by placing them in the right hands. Financially, it is not an easy trade because the most wanted books are not available: they cannot be ordered from anywhere, and the number of readers is always a small proportion of the public, and a particularly impoverished proportion at that. But the books come and go. We manage to keep paying the bills.

Most humour is at someone's expense, and this collection is no exception, but I have tried to poke fun at both sides of the counter. It is difficult to believe what people get up to in bookshops, but I now know that the world is full of silly clots, and that we seem to congregate around books.

Put another way, the world of books is infested with book-worms, and we leave our droppings everywhere!

The anecdotes without an acknowledgement were collected by myself during eight years experience at Goldmark Books in Uppingham, the second town of the old county of Rutland. I may be biased, but the fact that *so many* quotations have come from that lovely shop must mean that there is something special about the place. Interpret that how you will. We've learnt everything by making mistakes and always preferred to laugh rather than cry!

Frustrated sales first inspired me to start collecting anecdotes of impossible requests or absurd excuses for not buying. When other bookdealers heard about my collection they sent me their own favourites for inclusion, and these are all acknowledged except for those from two dealers who wished to remain anonymous. It is only fair to add that the general style and philosophy of the book is my own responsibility, and not necessarily in accord with the tastes or opinions of the other contributors.

"I suppose you get most of your books from people who have died!"
The Cavern, Haslemere.

1 GENERAL OBSERVATIONS

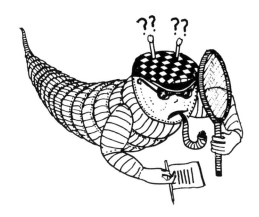

"Err, second-hand books! I bought one once but I didn't like it."

"Do you sell books?"
Room at the Top, Kingsbridge, Devon.

"Do you deal in second-hand books?"

"Ah, now, this looks like a bookshop!"

"Oh, you've got some books! They take some sorting out, don't they, take some sorting out. You know, you've got some books here I've never even seen before. I've not even seen them advertised! They take some sorting out. Are you open Sundays?"

"What *are* books? Where do they come from?"

"I've said it once, and I'll say it again: *nice to have a book in the house*, especially if you want to get to sleep at night, a few paragraphs should suffice."

"That book is obviously from the same library as the other."
Oh, how's that?
"The dust on the top is the same."

"It smells very bookie in here!"

"Do you make books?"
Nial Devitt Books, Leamington Spa.

"I had a book myself once. Never read it. It was blue. I don't suppose you've got a copy?"

"I don't know how you can bear to sell them!"
Mrs. A. Kent (Books), Framlingham.

"We love books. We spend all our time in bookshops. But I wish we had more time to spend today."
The constant plea of those who only come once and never stay for more than ten minutes.

"Choose me a book!"

"Are you a bibliophile?"

THAT·BOOK·IS·WINKING·AT·ME·

"I can't read novels, there's too many facts I still don't know so I haven't got time."

"My wife paints."
Goldmark Gallery, Uppingham.

"You've opened up a whole new world to me! I now collect modern first editions, but tell me, do you know what 'new impression' means?"
Graham Hodge, Wellingborough.

13

"I see you've put all the paperbacks in alphabetical order by author, but why can't you put them in title order as well?"
Room at the Top, Kingsbridge.

"May we come in and look round and go out without buying anything?"
Determined non-buyers at Margaret Pole's, Thaxted.

"Oh, I like that piece of music you're playing. I've heard it on a TV advert. Who wrote it?"
Well, it's by Bach, Sir.
"Oh, has he written any other pieces for television?"
Not that I know of . . .
Just Books, Truro.

"What d'yer call them, then, 'antiquarian'?"
Books Etc., Stamford.

"My dear, what a place for a book-worm to linger!"
Margaret Pole, Thaxted.

"Gee, that was published a hundred years before we had a president!"

"You've got a lot of gardening books, I wish I was more interested in gardening . . . You won't believe this when I tell yer – I've never read a book in my life . . . but I am interested in *Cooking With Cheese*, oh but it's got meat recipes in it too . . . ah, I could do with a new Atlas, mine's forty years old, but I'll need one with the whole world in it . . ." etc.
Customer on a very quiet Wednesday afternoon, who also told me she was a teacher!

14

"This book was rather a waste of tree, wasn't it?"

"Have you been to Oxford recently? I went there myself last week. I always does well at Bakewells." [*sic*]

"It hasn't got the golf course on it!"
Customer viewing the 1635 Blaeu map of Rutland.

"Normally, of course, I don't buy my books second-hand, if you see what I mean."

"Myself, I'm in publishing."
That's interesting. Which company?
"Oh, top-end stuff. Mitchell Beazley, actually."

"What an excellent collection of books you have – just right for an elderly middle-brow like myself!"
Margaret Pole, Thaxted.

"Hello, how are you? You're not sold out yet I see."

"My father-in-law lent me a copy of this book on *Marine Engineering* because I was doing a course on car maintenance and he thought it might be helpful."
Cheyne Lane Bookshop, Stamford.

"I've thrown better books than that out! Me and Billy belong to a book-club, you know."
The Bookshop, Belfast.

"What a life you people lead!"

The more enthusiastic someone's behaviour in a shop, the less he or she is actually interested:
"Oh, second-hand books! Look, Tony, these are all second-hand. Have you got any science fiction? What about fossils?"
[*I actually bothered to show some old books on fossils.*]
"Yes, I think those are a bit too advanced. We must come again . . ."
Never even looked at our large science fiction section!

"Oooohhhhh, a Bookshop!"
Overheard through the open door on a warm day; needless to say, she didn't come in.

"Oh, I do so love old books! Mind you, I've never actually read a book in my life!"
Customer in search of knitting patterns at Books and Chattels, Ludlow.

"I expect you've got them all computerised!"

This pair didn't buy anything either:
"Oh, look, a book on The National Gallery! Oh, Charles Dickens! Oh look, they've got a Repton! Look, a Repton. How much is your Repton?" (*£200, Madam*) "Oh. Now what's that, can't quite make it out: S.H.A.K.E.S.P.E.A.R.E. Isn't that marvellous? Oh, how wonderful! Ah, Holbein's Drawings! You know we've got Venetia's granny staying for Christmas? She's sweet. Crown Jewels! By Sitwell! Oh, look, a book about my hero! Oh, marvellous darling, who's your hero? Sir Walter Scott. How lovely! Oh look, James Lees Milne! Oh, he's so scurrilous, darling!"

16

THEY·ALL·WENT·ON·THE·BONFIRE . . . . .

"My aunt used to have a whole set of these, but they all went on the bonfire after she died."
Nicholas Willmott, Ipswich.

"We don't keep books in the house – such a fire risk!"
The Cavern, Haslemere.

17

"I've got a copy of that at home!"
How fascinating . . .

"Are these books for sale, or are they your own collection?"
The Observatory, Sitka, Alaska.

"I think I've found my 84 Charing Cross Road!"
Books Etc., Stamford.

"We've got a lovely book at home. It's full of marvellous colour pictures. It's all about, err, Hitler."

Customer after spending an hour browsing:
"Have you had a history buy recently?"
Yes.
"The history section is looking terrific at the moment – I must come back again when I've got more time."
Never seen him before or since!

"I expect you do a lot of trade with the public schools."
Yes, I can think of at least five masters who read.

"There's nothing like a good book that smells!"

"All his own work!"
The headline in a local newspaper carrying an article on our major exhibition of the work of Michael Ayrton.

"I like the frame . . ."
Goldmark Gallery.

IT'S·A·LOVELY·JOB·YOU'VE·GOT, SORTING·ALL·THESE

"I'm not a bookworm, but I know what I like."
Overheard from outside the door.

"Are there any single books which are worth a lot? What do books go up to, then?"

"Come on, drink your coffee, this browsing's not doing us any good at all."

"Gosh, this place is tidy! What's the matter?"

19

"And now, I'm going to get on the floor! Elephants at play! Now, *The Culture of the Abdomen* by Hornibrook . . . Yes, I think I'll have that. We'll see if I can cultivate an even larger one."
Stout customer of Margaret Pole, Thaxted.

"Mmm. It's a good idea these bookshops." [*American lady*]

"Come on, it's only books."
Two men who stood inside the door for a few seconds.

"What are we doing in here? I've got a chest-full of books at home. My grandfather was a reader."

"You won't have time to write your own poetry if you read anyone else's."
Wife to husband.

Pompous Englishman on holiday abroad:
"Ah, I remember when that book was very common, used to sell for 7/6d."
The Observatory, Sitka, Alaska.

"Are you the front desk here?"

"Do you like keeping a library?"
Mrs A. Kent (Books), Framlingham.

"Shall we go in here?"
"I might if it's one of the more organised ones . . ."
Overheard from outside the door at The Cheyne Lane Bookshop, Stamford.

"What d'ye want to buy him that for? Sure, he's already got a book."
The Bookshop, Belfast.

A little face suddenly appeared round the door, very low down, about level with the door handle. In beautifully modulated tones, very like those of Ermintrude on *The Magic Roundabout*, it said: "Just having a peep." Then it was gone. The place could have been full of margarine for all the old dear saw of it.
The Book Nook, Fort William.

"Eee, you can tell by the feel a good book, can't you?"

"I've lived here all my life and never noticed you before."
The Book Nook, Fort William, two weeks after opening.

"I do so love the smell of old books."
Nicholas Willmott, Ipswich.

"I just came on the spur of the moment, but I'm not really in the mood for choosing books."
SPCA Charity Bookshop, Malta.

"So, do people read books in your area, then?"
Ben Bass, Marshfield.

"How does it work? Do you have to join?"
Robert Humm, Stamford.

"I can tell this is a knowledgeable place. Some of my friends, you know, they don't even know what a shakespeare is!"

"You haven't many books, have you?"
Room at the Top, who have a stock of 20,000 books and as much again in their backstock.

YOU · HAVEN'T · MANY · BOOKS · HAVE · YOU ?

"You must get exhausted every Saturday night, clearing it all away ready for the service on Sundays."
Chapel Collector's Centre, Castor [a converted chapel].

"I study Puck."
German lady buying a copy of Arthur Rackham's Midsummer Night's Dream.

"What an interesting stock you have! You really have quite a variety! Still, I must be going, thank you . . ."

I like the stones on your necklace, Madam.
"Yes, they're latrines, you know!"
Oban Antiques, Oban.

"I thought I would read it in here, and then, if it is any good, my local library could get it for me . . ."
G. K. Hadfield, Shepshed.

"Oh, old prints! They look all right on the first day, but you soon realise they're nothing."
Uppingham Gallery.

"By, some of these are well written. You can tell they're by bookish people."

"I'm still buying something, even when the entire stock is utterly moribund."
Customer buying a 75p Terry Wogan paperback!

"By, your prices are reasonable! I must come again when I've got more time."

"Mmm. Not very good quality stock is it?"

"We had a book in the house when I were a girl!"
Beck Head Books, Kirkby Lonsdale.

"It must be lovely to sit here all day doing nothing."
Mrs. A. Kent (Books), Framlingham.

"Are your books in any kind of order?"

"This is the place where the man makes ornaments!"
Blissfully unappreciative customer of The Sculptor Studio, Uppingham.

"I can't imagine how you people make a living."
A parson at Mr. Badger's Bookshop, Taunton.

"What a nice job – no hard work, just sit back and take the money."
Room at the Top, Kingsbridge.

Spiritualist lady holding up a copy of a book which contained a picture of a long-dead First World War soldier:
"You see him! He's my helper!"

"I'm ever so sorry, I must owe you an awful lot of money."
Really, why's that?
"Well, I've had these out so long, the fines must be huge by now . . ."

"Your shop smells of cats!"
Yes, Sir, he's called Splodge.

"Mills and Boon are so satisfying."
SPCA Charity Bookshop, Malta.

We once had a wonderful window display of books on Japan and Japanese art, but this did not stop someone putting his head round the corner and saying:
"I just thought I'd let you know that I'm not at all interested in books on Japan!" *And out he went!*

"Do you keep the books on your shelves indefinitely?"

"Yes, I know you're a bookseller, but what do you really do?"
Louise McDermott, Rome, Italy.

"Matthew Arnold! He was the one who shot the President, wasn't he?"
Columbine Books, Southampton.

"By, you must be so clever, working here, having read all these!"

Two American ladies who selected two leather-bound books, one of Coleridge, the other of Milton:
"Oh, gee, aren't these cute? But who was this guy Milton anyway?"
Well, among British poets, Madam, we rank him second only to Shakespeare.
Other Lady: "Gee, well, I reckon you got the best of the two bargains."

We have the list of titles ready for you. Would you like me to pop it round?
"Is it a long list?"
Well, it's about twenty items . . .
"I suppose I had better collect it from you, then."

"Do you belong to this shop?"
The Bookshop, Belfast.

Customer leaving requests:
"They might be a bit cagey when you ring and ask for me, so just tell them it's about books and they'll put you through."
Oh, really, what do you do for a living?
"Err, ah, well, I don't really mind telling you. I work for Militant Tendency actually, but now that I've been expelled from the Labour Party I may as well be a bit more honest about it!"

"Do you mind if I have my breakfast?"
Christopher Williams, Poole.

DO·YOU·MIND·IF·I·HAVE·MY·BREAKFAST·?

"Oh, that's a nice old map. Do you know who the choreographer was?"
Louis Leopold, March.

"Could I have a look round your basement?"
Yes, of course, but what are you looking for?
"Stick insects."
Ah . . .

"Eee, now then. Fancy all that money for a picture with holes in it!"
Customer admiring a modern reproduction of a Leonardo da Vinci cartoon, at Beck Head Books, Kirkby Lonsdale.

"Do you live here?"
The Observatory, Sitka, Alaska.

Three old ladies admiring with great enthusiasm a book called Summer Souvenirs, *a book of colour photographs of nice young men in swimming trunks, etc., lying on beaches, etc.:*
"Oh, look at that! Oh, he's nice! Hey (giggle, giggle), look at him! But, they're all dressed . . ."

"I can see you're the absolute sort for doing books. The absolute!"
Really, and what do you do for a living?
"I'm a V.A.T. inspector."

"We'll try round the corner now and see what the real bookshop's got to offer."

"So, how did you hurt your neck?"
Oh, I did it in my sleep.
"Really? Do you have vivid dreams?"
Yes, sometimes.
"Ah, I think I know what must have happened, then. It must have been your spiritual body slipping away from your physical during the night, and then not being able to get back properly. I can dematerialise too, you know. Would you like me to appear in your bedroom one night?"

"Oh! Isn't this the Halifax Building Society?"
Just Books, Uppingham.

"Is there a recommended age at which books become valuable?"

Two old ladies, outside the window:
"Now then, 'Antiquarian', what does that mean?"
"Oh, I know! It means 'underwater'!"
Robert Vaughan, Stratford-upon-Avon.

Wife: "What's 'topography' mean?"
Husband: "Oh, it's cutting hedges into fancy shapes . . . I think."
Overheard at Beck Head Books, Kirkby Lonsdale.

"Well, you're certainly getting some doorstops in nowadays!"

"I never buy second-hand books – one never knows where they've been."
Wyrd Book Company, Saxmundham.

"What do people come in here for?"
Occultique, Northampton.

"There's something bookie in the air today!"

THREE SECOND-HAND COMMENTS
OF FRIENDS OF CUSTOMERS:

"I'm not going in there again! It's the most filthy, disgusting hole I've ever been in!"

"I just can't enjoy going in that shop, it's full of books!"

"I daren't go in there, they might offer me a cup of coffee!"

"The true value of a book is calorific."
Mike Goldmark.

Weren't you into shooting, Sir?
"Oh, yer, I do all the natural history things."
Books Etc., Stamford.

2 SPECIFIC REQUESTS

"Do you have a first edition Shakespeare? I was offered a first in Melbourne, but this is nearer to where he was born, isn't it?"
M. & R. Glendale, London.

"There's a few articles I want to read in the *Encyclopaedia Britannica*. Could you buy one in for me so I could have a look at it?"

"Do you have *No Mean City*?"
No, I'm sorry, not at the moment.
"Oh. It's out of print in Glasgow but I thought it might be in print in here."
The Book Nook, Fort William.

"Got any books on Egypt? It's them big stone things which appeal to me. I can just imagine my kids running riot on them!"

"Hey, Harv. They got George Eliot! Now, there's a guy who could write books."
American customer of Dave Jackson, Gloucester.

"I started collecting the book in weekly parts. You've got it, but it seems completely different!"

"Have you got the Lusitania?"
It sank, Madam.
"Yes, I know that, but have you got it?"
No, Madam.
"Well, we'll try the other bookshop, but we might come back to you."

"I'm a very keen collector of illustrated books. I always buy ones by Rackman [*sic*]. Do you have any?"

"Do you hunt?"
No, Madam.
"Do you fish?"
No, Madam.
"Do you shoot?"
No, Madam.
"Well, what do you do?"
Well, I read the occasional book.
"Oh really! Have you read *The Virgin Soldiers*?"
This happened to one of our customers at a Hunt Ball.

"What are those up there?"
Ah, that is a very fine reading set of Dickens, Sir.
"Oh, really, nice to have a bit of Shakespeare in the house."

"Have you got any books on bomb-making? It's for my son's school project."
The Bookshop, Belfast.

"Do you hire out sunbeds?"
Honest, it did happen!

"I be looking for an old book on Devon. It be red."
Mr. Badger's Bookshop, Taunton.

"Oh, do you not sell fish?"
Border Bookshop, Todmorden.

"I'm looking for a book. I forget the name of the author, but I know that she wrote it under her pudendum . . ."
Ben Bass, Marshfield.

"I'd like a really good book to get my teeth into. Have you any starting-to-read ones?"
Room at the Top, Kingsbridge.

"Do you have any books bound in human skin?"
Nial Devitt Books, Leamington Spa.

"Have you any books for sitting down and reading, not for study?"

"Excuse me, but, do you rent-out second-hand baking tins?"
Blitzgeist Bookshop, Birmingham.

"Have you got a copy of *Catcher in the Rye?*"
Not at the moment, but you could try the other bookshop in the next street.
"Why, do they have one?"
The Bookshop, Belfast.

"Mmm, I like cowboys . . ."

"A colleague of mine at Leicester University has just heard that there's a marvellous bookshop here in Uppingham, and he asked me if I could get him a list of all your stock."
[*How long would it take to write out 100,000 titles?*]

"What's the weirdest, whackiest book you've got?"
Occultique, Northampton.

"I only read books about wild animals and nuns – they're so restful."
The Cavern, Haslemere.

"Do you have any Gerry Anderson material?"
Not at the moment, but I'll see if I can pull a few strings for you.

"Do you know anything about cassette recorders?"
The Bookshop, Belfast.

"Do you have anything on occupational folklore?"
C.E.B. Mawson, while at Foyles, London.

"Have you got any Barbara Cartland? She's as good as the others, isn't she?"

"I wonder, could you tell me where Kate Greenaway lives? We like her work so much we'd like to commission her to decorate the bathroom."
Bertram Rota, London.

"Have you got any books with paintings on the foreskin?"
The pen-is mightier than the sword?

"Do you have any old Trollope here?"

"I bought this here three years ago and I've come in to change it!"
The Bookshop, Blakeney.

I once had a beautiful book you would have liked, but it got stolen . . .
"Oh, I've got that."
They never listen to what we're saying! Overheard at Books Etc., Stamford.

"Have you anything by Metal Arse?"
The customer meant Grace Metalious. SPCA Charity Bookshop, Malta.

"Can you direct me to your department specialising in medieval manuscripts, preferably illuminated?"

"I'm looking for books on the cult of the Black Virgin in Southern France in the eighth century . . ."
C.E.B. Mawson, while at Foyles, London.

"Is it OK to get a haircut here?"
Blitzgeist Bookshop, Birmingham.

"I think I now prefer them red ones [*she meant the 'Silhouette Desire' series*] 'cause there's more detail in them."
What do you mean?
"I'm not telling you!"

"Are your Agatha Christie in any particular order?"
The Bookshop, Belfast.

"Have you any poetry books in suede covers?"
Books and Chattels, Ludlow.

"Have you got a copy of *Shropshire Lad*?"
No, I'm afraid we haven't at the moment . . .
"Oh, that's a pity because I'm quite partial to them."

"Got any old Burkes?"

"Have you anything else like that, sort of novelist thing?"

"Have you got a copy of Bernard Shaw's *The Harmless Man*?"
Andrew Stewart, Helpringham.

"Where do you keep the time-switches for three-pin plugs?"
Blitzgeist Bookshop, Birmingham.

"I realise that you specialise in music, but, I wonder, do you have any books on motorcycles?"
Travis & Emery, related by Nicholas Willmott, Ipswich.

"I'd like a pot of double cream, please."
Lady who hadn't realised that the shop had changed from a dairy to a bookshop two years before.
County Bookshop, Oakham.

STILL · GOT · THAT · MOUNTAINEERING · BOOK ?

"Whatever happened to that mountaineering book I reserved a year ago? I'd spend some money if you found it for me."

"Have you got a copy of *New Austrian Tunnelling Methods*?"
No, I don't think so at the moment, Sir . . .
"Well, what about *Swedish Blasting Techniques*, then?"
C.E.B. Mawson, while at Foyles, London.

"Have you any true books – I'm not too keen on friction?" [*sic*]
The Bookshop, Belfast.

"How much is your plant?"
Beck Head Books, Kirkby Lonsdale.

"Le Carré? Ain't he the guy that wrote *The Poseidon Adventure*?"
No, that was Paul Gallico.
"Yeah? Gee, I always get those Frenchies mixed up."
Dave Jackson, Gloucester.

"Do you stock Kendal Mint Cake?"
Mrs. A. Kent (Books), Framlingham.

"Isn't this the Tourist Information Office?"
Books Etc., Stamford.

"Is this the place where I can get my false teeth fixed?"
Books Etc., Stamford.

"Do you sell Walls Ice Cream or is it just a shop?"
Books Etc., Stamford.

"Oh, I was looking for the Council Office. I've got to report a death."
Books Etc., Stamford.

Customer holding a copy of Hamlet:
"Is Shakespeare in this?"
The Bookshop, Belfast.

SOON · GET · THEM · BUGGERS · OUT . . .

"Got any books with them vinegarettes in?" [*sic*]
Well, one or two . . .
"Good, soon get them buggers out . . ."

Print Dealer:
"Have you a copy of Throsby's *Select Views in Leicestershire*? I've
always wanted to break one of those!"

"Do you have a book on how owners look like their dogs?"
Peter Skinner, New York.

"Excuse me, but would you mind telling me what my husband was looking for?"

"I was here last year and you had a book on that shelf down there. Have you moved it?"
The Bookshop, Blakeney.

"I wonder, do you ever come across any art books?"

"I can't remember what the book's called, but it's by a man!"
Jeroby Books, Oadby.

Customers often like to impress booksellers by using long words where short ones will do, often in the hope that the dealer will not know what it means so that they can have the pleasure of explaining. And sometimes they get it wrong:
"Have you got anything on hornithology?"

"Do you have anything on cucurbits?"

"Do you have a book on Ekistics?"
C.E.B. Mawson, while at Foyles, London.

"Campanology?"
Well, we have a few books on gay rights . . .
"It's about bell-ringing!"
Err, yes, of course, that's what I meant.

"Got any books on gazebos?"

American customer:
"Do you have a festive restroom?"
I'm sorry..?
"A festive restroom . . ."
I'm sorry, I just don't understand what you mean.
"All right, where's y'u toilet?"

"Do you have a comfort station?"

Discreet American talking in hushed tones in very quiet shop:
"Do you have a restroom?"
A restaurant? No I'm afraid not, Sir. If I had I'd park my Rolls Royce outside. Do you want me to recommend one?
"Yes."
Would you like an expensive one?
"All right . . . err, do you have a bathroom?"
A bathroom? No, we don't have one of those here. If you want a bath, I suppose you need an hotel.

"Is this the chemist?"
Mrs A. Kent (Books), Framlingham.

"Do you have any sort of speciality?"
Well, not really, we're a general bookshop, but there are three of us here, and we each have our own interests.
"Really, and what's your line?"
Well, I'm specially interested in medieval history . . . [so I showed him our six shelves of medieval history]
"This is all on Chaucer, is it?"
No, it's on medieval studies in general.
He looked for a while and then said:
"You'll be building it up, will you?"
Some people you just can't please.

"Are *Readers' Digest* books collectable?"

IT'S · THE · EXPERIMENTS · YOU · KNOW..

Very strange customer holding up a copy of a History of the Nazi SS, and nudging me as he did so:
"I'll have this if I may, the experiments you know . . ."

"Do you have any good children's books?"
It depends how you define good.
"Well, you know, the sort that you wouldn't normally give to them."
Err, I don't quite . . .
". . . Like early editions of *Little Black Sambo*."

45

"Have you got anything that pulls out, pops up or waves about?"
Titles, Oxford.

"Is this the greengrocer?"
No, Sir, we're a bookshop.
"Oh, well, do you have any lip salve, then?"
Jermy and Westerman, Nottingham.

"It's a thick paperback with a red spine; have you got it?"
SPCA Charity Bookshop, Malta.

"Have you anything soppy enough for my grandmother for Christmas? I don't want to have to swallow my pride and get her a Barbara Cartland."

"Where do I get a copy of the book which tells me what second-hand books are worth? You know, like the one on cars."
Nial Devitt Books, Leamington Spa.

"I got your catalogue this morning, but the book I want isn't in it! It's got two swans in it. Do you have it?"
Green Meadow, Kinoulton.

"I'm looking for a particular book – I forget the title and who wrote it, but I'd know it if you showed it to me."
The Bookshop, Belfast.

"I don't like stories. I prefer my books to have facts in them. Preferably chemistry facts."

"Do you sell stamps?"
Norman Lord, London.

"Have you got any Jeffrey Archer? It's not for me, I go for the big red or blue books myself."

"Have you any first edition Dickens?"
Jeffrey Archer himself when he visited us.

"Have you got any old new books?"

I had just opened the door, hadn't even put the lights on, when I was aware that someone had come in behind me. In broad Glaswegian he says: "Dae ye sell books here, Jimmy?" Refraining from the natural sarcastic reply that sprang to mind I said yes. "Right," he said and took one at random off the nearest shelf. I think it was chemistry or physics. "I'll have that one." And he paid up and went off happily.
The Book Nook, Fort William.

"It had a large colour picture of an octopus, do you know it?"
SPCA Charity Bookshop, Malta.

"No, Mills and Boon are too heavy for me, I want something a bit lighter."

"Have you got *Rupert Bear Number Thirteen?*"
No, I don't think so at the moment . . .
"Well, you're too young to remember them anyway."

"Have you got any biographies that aren't boring?"
SPCA Charity Bookshop, Malta.

"Do you have a book on the pyramids? It's by a woman."
Peter Skinner, New York.

"Where do you keep the tins of tomato soup?"
Well, actually we're a bookshop, Madam, but we could perhaps sell you a book which would tell you how to make it.
"Oh, you stupid dealers, you never know anything!"
Nial Devitt Books, Leamington Spa.

THE · VIOLENT · FAIRY

"I'm looking for a copy of *The Violent Fairy Book*."
Nicholas Willmott, Ipswich.

"How many books are there in Olivia Manning's *Levant Trilogy?*"
Leicester University Bookshop, reported by Barbara Latham.

49

"Where is your Latvian department, please?"
Oh, I'm sorry, but we don't have any.
"Well, where in Stratford can I buy Latvian books?"
Robert Vaughan, Stratford-upon-Avon.

"I'm looking for a book called *Hashish*. Err, it's a serious anthropological text."
C.E.B. Mawson, while at Foyles, London.

"I'm not sure of the author or publisher . . ."
Well, try us, you never know.
"It's called *Poland*."

"Dear Sir,
Thank you for your catalogue. Please could you reserve item no. 12. I would be grateful if you would first send me a rubbing of the binding, for which I enclose a pencil and paper, and a stamped and addressed envelope."
Andrew Stewart, Helpringham.

"Have you got *Anne of Clark Gables*?"
The Bookshop, Belfast.

"Have you a catalogue for the military museum in Paris?"

"Have you got any Bibles?"
Yes, any particular translation?
"No, not a translation, I want the original!"
Oh, I don't think we've got any Greek or Hebrew texts at the moment . . .
"I don't want them, I want the original, the English one . . ."
I think you mean the King James version. Yes, we do have one, but I think you'll find that God spoke Hebrew, not English . . .

"Have you got any of them books by Vidal Sassoon?"

"Where do you keep scientific books, James Hadley Chase and Earl Stanley Gardner? Why don't you put them all together?"
SPCA Charity Bookshop, Malta.

"I'm very keen on human and animal interaction in Andalusia. Got anything for me?"
C.E.B. Mawson, while at Foyles, London.

"It's by that woman with a funny name . . ."
Jeroby Books, Oadby.

"If it's a man's book you're looking for, Wilbur Smith is an excellent writer."
Err, I'm not so sure . . .
"Oh, it's got everything in it."

"I'd like a copy of *Moby Dick*. I don't mind who it's by."

"I want something to really get my teeth into, but nothing heavy."
SPCA Charity Bookshop, Malta.

"Have you got a copy of *The Female Enoch*?"
Nicholas Willmott, Ipswich.

"Have you got a copy of *Offa's Dykes*?"
C.E.B. Mawson, while at Foyles, London.

"Where would you put books that are just general but jolly interesting?"

"Do you have any ancient Bibles?"

No, I'm afraid not; not particularly ancient ones, anyway. Are you specially interested in theology, then?

"Sure! I'm a Baptist preacher, from Florida, U.S. of A. I was born again thirty years ago, and I also deal in ancient Bibles. The last one I bought was a manuscript, a Wycliffe. I sold it for £33,000."

Do you know, it's always struck me as being rather bizarre that a book which teaches that the love of money is the root of all evil should in itself command such a high price. Does seem to be rather contradictory, doesn't it?

"No, it's not, you're just SPIRITUALLY IGNORANT!"

And he walked out. What an interesting chap.

"Are you a Jew?"

Well, err . . .

"I've got a present for you here. It's a copy of the New Testament, translated into Hebrew. You should read this for your spiritual salvation."

Well, that's really very sweet of you to offer to give me that, but, I'm ever so sorry, I'm just not interested.

"DO YOU MIND GOING TO HELL? BECAUSE THAT'S WHERE YOU'RE GOING!"

And, like the nice man from Florida, she walked out. What an interesting lady.

"Where do you keep the true crime fiction?"

Just Books, Uppingham.

"Do you sell books?"

Yes . . .

"Well, now I've forgotten the title or the author of the one I'm looking for, but could you please read out a few of your titles to see if they ring a bell?"

Alan Brett, London.

I'VE · GOT · THAT · ALREADY . . . . .

Vicar with expensive tastes:
"Have you any signed firsts by Shakespeare?"
Not at the moment I'm afraid.
"What about signed firsts of Jane Austen?"
No, we're right out of them.
"Milton?"
Only some early reprints, not signed firsts.
"Oh, that's a pity. Is there anything else you think I might like?"
Well, we have a signed first of the Bible . . .
"Oh, I've got that already."

"Ayme lewking fer bewks on sick . . ."
C.E.B. Mawson, while at Foyles, London.

"I want a book to excite me!"
Mole Bookshop, East Molesey.

"Have you anything by William le Kwex?"
Terry Hale and Martin Stone, Paris, France.

"Have you anything by Eliot?"
Yes, we have Middlemarch *and* Silas Marner.
"Oh, that's strange. I didn't know he wrote them as well as the vet books . . ."
Pomes Penyeach, Newcastle-under-Lyme.

"Have you got anything on the history and typology of the cream bun? I'm an expert, you know."
Woodstock Bookshop, Woodstock.

"I like the *Saturday Book*. They're always nicely produced, nice books *to feel*."

"Have you any books in those very attractive cloth bindings from the 1840s?"
You mean the sort with the very exact definition of letters, deeply in-laid in gold-leaf, with wonderful blind tooling, and those nice bevelled edges, sensuous surfaces, and all sorts of different types of cloth-grain?
"Err, yes . . ."
Yeh, I quite like them, too. Perhaps we should form a liberation group?

WIND

"But I only came in to get out of the wind!"
Fred Bettley, Richmond.

3 EXCUSES FOR NOT BUYING

Every bookseller has had the infuriating experience of customers who demand with great enthusiasm a particular book, only to come up with a weak excuse for not buying it when it is found. Sometimes the customer genuinely did not like the copy or failed to realise that the book was worth a lot, but often they come in for an ego-trip. They request obscure items to impress their friends, in full knowledge of the fact that you are neither likely to have heard of it nor to have it in stock. Then the excuses flow . . .

"Have you got anything by Oscar Wilde?"
Were you looking for something in particular?
"Yes, *De Profundis* . . ."
Oh, I don't think we've got a copy at the moment, but I'll have a look . . . Ah yes, we do have a copy!
"Well, what I was really looking for was the Complete Works."

"This is exactly what I wanted: but it's so, sort of, school-text-book-ish."

"I'll not take anything this time. There's too many to pick from."
The Bookshop, Belfast.

"I must come back again when I've got my glasses with me."

An interesting customer was the one who hummed Wagner loudly while in our shop, because the boss overheard him in two other shops before he came in ours. First The Rutland Bookshop:
"Have you got Bridge's Northamptonshire?" [*A £200 item*]
No, not here, but we do have one in our other branch. Would you like us to bring it here for you?
"No, I don't think so."
Oh, it wouldn't be any trouble at all, honestly.
"No, I think I'll leave it. My friend's got one."
The boss then followed him into the Uppingham Gallery and overheard another conversation:
"Have you a Speed of Nottinghamshire?" [*Another £200 item*]
Yes we have, a very fine copy, here it is!
"Very nice, I think we'll leave it though, there'll be another one some time."
And then he came into our shop and asked:
"Antiquarian psychology? Have you any?"
No, not at the moment, apart from this interesting little item . . .
"Mmm. I think I'll leave it. Now there's an antique shop next door, isn't there . . .?"

"Have you got a copy of *Spycatcher*?"
I know where to get hold of one, Sir.
"Really? Still, I expect I shouldn't really buy it."

"No, I just couldn't see anything at all."

"Well, no, not at that price. I'm an artist myself so I could easily paint one at home."
Beck Head Books, Kirkby Lonsdale.

"No, I can't afford it. I bought a book last week . . ."

"I seem to have read all those."
M. & R. Glendale, London.

"Have you got a copy of *The Last Days of White Rhodesia* by David Hill, published by Chatto and Windus?"
Yes, I think we might . . . Yes, here we are, published at £8.95, our price £4.
"Err, yes. Now, I've just spent something next door in the antique shop, so I haven't any cash on me . . ."
Oh, that doesn't matter, we'll take a cheque . . .
"I bet you would . . ."
Or if you like, you can take the book with you and pay us when you're passing next . . .
"Err, look, I think I'd better ask my husband, it's for a friend you know. She was there. I wasn't in Rhodesia myself at the time, BUT IT'S WONDERFUL TO KNOW THAT YOU'VE GOT IT!"

"Thank you very much; we've had a lovely look round and really enjoyed your coffee; and we'll come again."

"It's wicked when you have to be so selective, isn't it?"

"Well, I'll have to ask my husband . . ."
The Observatory, Sitka, Alaska.

"What a pity I'm not studying Edwin Lutyens' architecture."

"I've been using a copy which belongs to a friend of mine for the last three years, and I've been looking for my own copy for the last twelve years. It's the *History of the King's Royal Volunteer Rifles*. You haven't by any chance got one, have you?"
Well, look no longer! I have one. Here you are . . .
"TWENTY-FIVE POUNDS! Oh, I never pay that for a book. Goodbye."
Books Etc., Stamford.

"That's a book I've been looking for for ages, but I came down town to put money in the bank, not to spend it."
The Bookshop, Belfast.

There was a customer who wanted a book called Tales of the Mountain Gunners. *We rang the publisher but there was no answer. We rang again – wrong number. We rang again – same wrong number. We rang Directory Enquiries and got a new number. We rang that and the operator interrupted us to tell us that the number had just been changed. We rang the new number (in Edinburgh) and they said 'Ring back later because the lady who deals with the books is having lunch.' We rang later and they told us that the book was out-of-print. So we then rang the customer and offered to advertise for a copy in the second-hand trade magazines, to which he replied:*
"Thank you, but you will ring me to check the price first – I don't want to pay a lot for it."

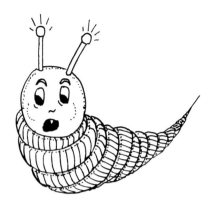

"Have you seen the print of the Quorn Hunt across the road?"
Yes, I have.
"It's £325!"
Yes . . .
"Well, don't you think that's rather a lot?"
Not really. I think that's probably about right.
"Oh, well do you think you could get one cheaper for me?"
I doubt it . . .
"Well, never mind. My mother has one. I'll just have to hope that she dies soon."
Uppingham Gallery.

"That's an old book, darling; it's terribly dirty too."
Wife to husband who was enjoying looking at a beautiful copy of Wright's Rutland *(1684).*

"Still, it's the difficulty of finding space on the bookshelf, isn't it?"
Why enquire at all if you haven't got room? A monumentally stupid statement from a customer at Books Etc., Stamford.

"What we really wanted was a matching pair for either side of the fireplace . . ."
Customer who had borrowed three watercolours to try out in her home.

"Yes, very nice, but my husband could probably buy that himself from another shop."

"Thank you very much. I've had a good look round and there were one or two which interested me . . ."
As leaving.

"There's a . . . book. Can't remember the title or what it was about. Err, I think it had a blue cover, it was here last time we were in."
Do you know the author, Sir?
"No."
Do you know where you saw it?
"No, it was about a year ago."
Well, I think we sold at least two books in the last year, so that must have been one of them.
"No, I don't think so because it was here the year before too. I didn't buy it then – I thought it was too much money."
Really, how much was it?
"£2."

"Oh, I was only looking at it because the title amused me. That's all."
Books Etc., Stamford.

"Thank you, there's one or two things, but err, I'm buying a new bookcase, and we're moving house to this area in two weeks, and once we get organised, there are one or two things, so we'll see you again."

"I think I'll leave it, but it's very good."

"By, your prices are reasonable. I must come again when I've got more time."

"Have you got a copy of *Little Dorrit*?"
Yes, here it is . . .
"Oh no, that's no good to me, it's far too long!"
Mrs A. Kent (Books), Framlingham.

"How much is it?"
It's nine pounds.
"Oh, I didn't realise it was a proper book."
Eunice Watkins, Maidstone.

"How much is this? Oh, 60p. Mmm. Well, I think I've got all that anyway."

"Oh books! Splendid! Well done! You know, there's a chap in our village who's a carpenter. Super chap! He'll make anything for you, from coffins to wheels. Ordinary, decent sort of chap, but he *wrote*! Marvellous little book. Do you know I've hunted everywhere for a copy. What I wouldn't give for a copy of that . . . Brown sort of book. Ordinary. Ordinary sort of chap, but I've never been able to find one."
Well, do you mean The Village Carpenter?
"Yes I do!"
In that case, it's your lucky day, we have a first edition.
"Oh . . . and how much is that?"
It's fifteen pounds, Sir.
"Oh God!"
And he ran out of the door!
The Rutland Bookshop, Uppingham.

"No, it was the blue one I wanted."

"No, I'm not paying that much. How can you charge a price like that for a picture that's only got two colours in it?"
Goldmark Gallery.

Can I sell you this book, Sir?
"Well, because I've already got a lot of books – more than most people – and due to the law of diminishing returns, there isn't really a lot of point in my buying another! I think I'll buy a tin-opener instead."

"Well, I've already got a full set anyway."
Books Etc., Stamford.

Would you like us to let you know when we get Scout books in?
"No, I'm an impulsive book-buyer, it's a terrible thing; but if I was to buy every book you mention to me, I'd soon have enough to set up in business in competition and you wouldn't like that would you? I'm sure there are plenty of people in Uppingham who are interested in that subject. Goodbye."

THERE'S · PLENTY · OF · PEOPLE · INTERESTED · IN · SCOUT · BOOK

"Do you have old geological books?"
Yes, we have a whole section full . . .
"Oh, marvellous, that's nice to know. I must come again when I've got more time . . . and is that really £100?"
Yes, it is.
"Marvellous, what a lovely book, and such good condition. Thank you so much, goodbye."

"Is there a lady here who speaks Welsh?"
No, Sir.
"Oh, that's a pity. I wanted a Welsh Bible."
Oh, we have one.
"Well, I really wanted a new one."

"Mmm, this *Mrs Beeton* is a bit expensive. You can get a modern one for much less than that, and it's much more up to date, you know."
Susan Taylor, Honley.

"Oh, we've got one black-and-white picture on the wall already."
Uppingham Gallery.

AN EXCUSE FOR NOT PAYING!

"Dear Miss Wesley,

I apologise for the delay in paying this invoice. However, in order for me to pay it, two things had to happen at the same time: (1) I had to be employed full-time, in order to have the money; and (2) I had to have access to the only post office that sells International Money Orders, or to one of the two banks that sell international bank drafts, and time to go there – not easy when you have only half an hour for lunch.

I would gladly have paid a little extra for exchange of my cheque, and you would have it sooner.

However, I finally got an International Money Order, and the post office is sending it."
Jacqueline Wesley, London.

CAN · I · FLOG · BOOKS · HERE?

4 BUYING AND SELLING
(and, Haggling over Price . . .)

"Do you buy books or just sell them?"

"How much do you pay for books?"

"Can you price this for me – I'd like to buy it."
Mmm, I'm not sure, but I think about £8.
"Oh, I've only got fifteen pence."

"My husband has just left me, so you can have these motoring books. Now, can you suggest something for the weekend?"
Mole Bookshop, East Molesey.

"Look, I'd like to buy these two paperbacks, but there's just one problem."
Oh, what's that?
"Well, this one says 25p inside and the other says 35p."
Oh, well, I tell you what, you can have the pair for 60p.
"Oh, that's very kind of you, thank you very much, I'll take them."

"I've got this book 'ere. It's very old. It's called *Black Beauty* and it's by a horse . . ."

"I'm not paying £4 for a book that cost 2/6d!"
Parkington Books, Billingham.

"Six quid . . . SIX QUID!! You must be joking! Why, the paperback was £4.95 ten years ago!"
Richard Way, Henley-on-Thames.

Oh, I didn't realise you were allowed to read things like that in the RAF!
"We're not, that's why I'm selling it before anyone finds out. . . . . ."

"Are all your books the same price?"
Beck Head Books, Kirkby Lonsdale.

Husband: "That's a nice book, and cheap at £10. There's another copy in the second-hand bookshop down the road at £20."
Wife: "Yes, Darling, but let's go down the road – you don't know who's been handling the books in a place like this!"
Overheard by J. and G. Curtis, Hornsea, at a flea market.

"Now, bottom-rock price on this one I think!"

I LIKE·TO·PUT·SELLOTAPE·ON·THE·COVERS··

I was examining, with a view to purchase, a small collection of
reasonably useful books. Each had a dustwrapper and each
dustwrapper had been smothered in filthy, yellowed sellotape. The
vendor commented:
"I like to put sellotape on the covers, it keeps them nice and
fresh."
Nicholas Willmott, Ipswich.

"You can't trust these bookdealers. They just think of a number
and halve it!"
Parkington Books, Billingham.

Disappointed vendor:
"I don't understand, you say you want to buy books – after all a book's a book, isn't it? One's very much like another."
Pomes Penyeach, Newcastle-under-Lyme.

Mother buying 25p paperback:
"Come on Shane, I've spent enough. We'll go and get your video."
Peter Howard (Books), South Croydon.

"I'm sure you'd make more money if you gave the books away and charged for the coffee."
You're probably right there.

"I've found this, it's ever so old – look, it's 1910. I don't suppose you see many books of that age. What will you give me for it?"
I'm sorry, but I can't buy it, Madam, because it has no covers or spine, and all the illustrations have been taken out. I'm afraid it's not worth anything to me.
"But it's so old it must be worth something!"
Well, look at this . . . Here's a book of 1678.
"Really? Oh, that really is old!"
Room at the Top, Kingsbridge.

"Oh, that's too much – they're out of date!"
David Flint, Basingstoke.

"There's only one page missing!"
Banbury Bookshop.

"Well, after all, the guilty feelings go but the books remain."
Big spenders at Margaret Pole's, Thaxted.

I'LL · TAKE · IT · AS · IT'S · SO · CHEAP . . . .

"Do you give a discount? My bookseller at home always does."
Mrs. A. Kent (Books), Framlingham.

"This is a horrible book, but I better take it as it's so cheap."
Mr. Badger's Bookshop, Taunton.

"What are your books like in terms of their price structure?"
Lorien Books, Kirkmichael, Perthshire.

"I'd like to buy a nice book as a present. How much is that one?"
Oh, that's a lovely book! It's £16, Madam.
"Oh marvellous! Well, I think that one will do. Will you take a cheque?"
Yes, of course.
Customer writes out a cheque for sixty pounds.
Oh no, I'm sorry you've made a mistake, the book's only £16.
"Only sixteen? Oh, I think I'll leave it then."
A change from the usual at The County Bookshop, Oakham.

"I'd like to buy this book please, but do you mind if I leave the dust-wrapper?"

I'm sorry, Sir, but we've just run out of bags. Would a box do?
"No, not really. You couldn't by any chance persuade one of the other customers to part with their bag? I'll give you five pence for it if you do."
The Birmingham Bookshop.

"I've got an old Shakespeare at home with his photo at the front . . ."
Just Books, Truro.

"Would you like to buy some books, they were left over from our jumble sale?"
Banbury Bookshop.

"It's awful giving away John Bunyan, I wouldn't do it of course, only I have two copies. My husband was a lay preacher, you know."

"Oh, is that the standard price of Rubaiyats? I bought one at £12.50. It wasn't the same as this one, but it's worth £40 is it? Mmm."

"I have a lot of books to sell. Some of them are very old. One has the date 1932 written inside it."
Nicholas Willmott, Ipswich.

"Do you give a clerical discount?"
Clergyman claiming special privilege at R. F. G. Hollett & Son, Sedbergh.

"I don't want to buy this book, but would you mind if I took a picture out? I quite like this one!"
Room at the Top, Kingsbridge.

The Blitzgeist Bookshop, Birmingham, ran an advert in their local press offering a discount to geniuses, hermits, minotaurs, etc. This inspired a very nice, middle-class lady to prance into the shop and announce:
"I'm an oral sadist and I claim my discount!"

"How come this Penguin from the 1930s isn't priced at 5p? It was 6d when it first came out and 5p would be DOUBLE the price!"
Banbury Bookshop.

I'm sorry, Madam, but the book is not worth anything to me.
"Well, where should I take it to sell? Would you recommend I try Hatchards?"
Bibliopol, Northampton.

"Shall we compromise?"
Mrs A. Kent (Books), Framlingham.

"£10 seems a lot, it was 12/- new!"
SPCA Charity Bookshop, Malta.

"Look here, you have charged my wife more than the price on the book-jacket!"
David Flint, Basingstoke.

"Is this a library or are the books for sale?"
Christopher Williams, Poole.

"Have you a book on parrots?"
I think I've got just the one . . .
"Oh, well, if you've only got one I'd better have it."
You'll find a much bigger selection over the road at the new bookshop.
"Oh, aren't these new? Are you a second-hand bookshop? I'll leave it, thank you. It's for a present."
Mr. Badger's Bookshop, Taunton.

I can offer you just ten pence each for these, I'm afraid, but this one's very nice. I can give you twenty pounds for that.
"Oh, I never realised it was so valuable! You can buy the others but I think I'll keep this one for the family."
Oh, it is tempting to be dishonest sometimes . . .

"Ah, now, this one's dated 1918!"
Vendors like to tell you all about the book before you turn it down. I suppose we need to have these things pointed out to us.

"And I suppose you got it at a jumble sale for 25 pence!"
Customer upset at the price of a Kate Greenaway first edition (£9) at Margaret Pole's, Thaxted.

"I wish to sell this pair of shoes. They're good ones; I've only worn them once."
Rebecca Dearman, Leicester.

GOOD · MORNING · VICAR !

"Would you mind giving me two receipts for those books? One for the full amount and one showing the discount you'll give me?" *Clergyman who spent about £175, as he was 'doing a bit of dealing', but who we knew had already changed the price of one book from £20 to £10. Our response was simple. We counted the book as £10, and gave him no discount. That way his dishonesty cost him more than he stood to gain!*

"If you don't sell your Greek lexicon in a year, let me know and I'll come back for it."

"It's very old – King James printed it!"
Vendor of a 1920s Bible at Nial Devitt Books, Leamington Spa.

"I've brought in this collection of books. I wondered – could you make a list of them for me and mark down how much each is worth? My wife wants to sell some of them to her friends, but she wants to know how much to charge them. You can make an offer for the ones left over, when I bring them back."

"Tell me, what price are first editions?"
Mr. Mullarney, Dublin.

"Do you get given all your books?"
Mrs. A. Kent (Books), Framlingham.

"I'll give you £2 for that, plus a present!"
No Sir, I want cash!
"No, I insist, you'll like the present!"
Disappears to the sound of our further protests, book in hand, and returns a few seconds later carrying a brace of duck.

"Fifteen pounds! And it's not even new."
M. & R. Glendale, London.

"But I only wanted it to read!"
Nial Devitt Books, Leamington Spa.

"Well, now that you've bought my books, can you lend me a pair of scissors?"
Yes, certainly, but why do you want them?
"I want to cut my name out of each book."
Bibliopol, Northampton.

"I thought I'd let you know – I've put sellotape all round the edges so they'll keep nice."
Green Meadow, Kinoulton.

Lady enters shop while proprietor is deeply involved with a Gavin Lyall thriller:
"Oh! If only I'd known! I've just bought three pairs of high heels as good as new, still with the price-stickers on . . ."
We buy and sell books, Madam.
". . . And a lovely pair of Dr. Martin's for my son, Kevin!"
We don't buy or sell shoes.
"If I'd known I'd have bought them here."
The Blitzgeist Bookshop, Birmingham.

"You've got to buy these books: I've got a taxi waiting outside and I haven't got the fare!"
The Bookshop, Belfast.

"I threw away all the wrappers because the books were so bright and shiny underneath!"
Mr. Badger's Bookshop, Taunton.

"How much are your Mills and Boon?"
They're twenty pence each, Madam.
"Oh! I thought you were selling them cheap."
The Bookshop, Belfast.

"Perhaps I'd better take them to an antiquarian bookseller."
Disappointed vendor of useless books at a Book Fair, reported by W. Musgrove, Plymouth.

"How much is your kettle?"
The Cavern, Haslemere.

"Can you do a bit off this one?"
Err, all right, we've had it for a while . . . £2: I'll do it for £1.50.
"Mmm, and this one? It says £3 but it once sold for £1!"
Well, prices do change.
"Mmm."
I'll do it for £2.75.
"No, I think I'll leave it."

Vendor of recent Book Club editions:
"Well they cost me a lot of money and I expect they've gone up since then!"
Columbine Books, Southampton.

"Let me say how much I appreciate your Anthony Gross exhibition – I've really enjoyed it!"
Oh, marvellous. Can I persuade you to buy the catalogue? There's lots of text and illustrations in it, and it's only £4.
"No, I don't need the catalogue, it would only get lost, and I've got plenty of his work at home to admire."
Goldmark Gallery.

Thank you, that's 75p please.
"It beats me how you can charge 75p when it says 50p on the back."
But that was in . . . 1972.
"Yes, but it still says it on the back."
Well, we have had 3, 4 or 500% inflation since then . . .
"Well . . ."
And if it's still in print I'm sure it would be more like £2.95.
"Oh, I'm sure it would be."
She paid with great reluctance. How much is Leon Uris worth?

"I overheard you giving a discount to the man before me. What will you knock off this one? It's marked at 25p."
Room at the Top, Kingsbridge.

"My wife and I have just taken up Scrabble, and we would like a good cheap dictionary . . ."

Well, we've got Chambers' Dictionary. I understand that that's recommended by the makers of Scrabble and it's only £4.99.

"Pah, no, a cheap dictionary!"

Well, how about Longman's Dictionary? That's only £3.50.

"No, I said I wanted a CHEAP dictionary!"

We've got the Concise Oxford at £2.50 . . .

"Far too much!"

This one's only 50p.

"Ah! Err, no, I couldn't possibly read the type of that one."

Yes, it's not very good is it. Now, err, how about this one: the Pocket Oxford at only £1.50. That's probably the best cheap dictionary we've got!

"Mmm. Yes, fine, we'll take that one. Err, discount for cash?"

Would you like a cup of coffee?

"I see you have a copy of *Churchill By His Contemporaries*. How much do you want for the dustwrapper?"

The Bookshop, Belfast.

"If I leave you a five bob deposit, could I return it tomorrow when I've finished reading it?"

Nial Devitt Books, Leamington Spa.

"How much do you pay for big books?"

Stephen Foster Books, Wandsworth.

"No, this is preposterous. I don't like the way I'm being treated! You must make out a list and specify the price you're offering for each one. This is not the way to dispose of one's life-long collection of theology."

"How much are your chairs?"

Hopeful vendor:
"I don't know anything about books to be honest, but that one I'll want £50 for, to be straight with yer. Ah come from an old farming family, you know, so we used to have books. They used to have books in them days, didn't they? Used to give them to each other . . ."

"Do you buy books that have been read?"
The Cavern, Haslemere.

Someone made a request for copies of the 'In Praise of . . .' series and a few Elizabeth Goudge novels. We quoted them three from the series at £1 each, and an Elizabeth Goudge paperback at 50p. They came in and bought the paperback only, so I asked "Are you not collecting the 'In Praise Of' series?" And they replied:
"Well, we were, but at £1 a time, I think it will be too expensive."

"Oh, but I thought someone would be interested in that. Surely they would, I've read it myself many times."
The constant plea of a regular who is known to be illiterate.

"I was going to throw these out but my neighbour said 'Why don't you try them at the bookshop?', but I said to her 'Surely they don't buy books?'"

"You're a miserable, stingy, tight-fisted beggar. I'll just have to take my books elsewhere to sell."
Oh do! I'm sure they'll bite your hands off!
"Well, there's no need to be nasty about it!"
The Bookshop, Belfast.

"I have a book at home about furniture. It was a pretty limited edition sort of thing. How much do you think it might be worth?"

"Now, little lady, let me teach you a thing or two about business.
Anybody ever tell you about cash-flow?"
M. & R. Glendale, London.

"Do you take credit cards?"
A tramp buying a 40p paperback at The Bookshop, Belfast.

"Can you explain to me why it is that this old Wisden's Almanack is worth £10, but old copies of Whitaker's are not worth much, even though they've got far more interesting facts in them, and more of them? Why?"
Well, Madam, it's the men you see, they like cricket and they like to keep a record of the scores . . .
"Oh, I see. Women just read Mills and Boon, don't they? When I was a librarian we used to have old copies of Wisdens but no new one, so I suggested to my friend at the library that she sell the old ones and buy a new Whitaker. I'm sure she could do that. Would you give her much for them?"
Well, probably not, because librarians usually destroy the books in their keeping by covering them in sellotape or rubber stamps . . .
"Oh, that reduces the value, does it?"

"I've never paid more than three pounds for a book."

A common saying often encountered when buying from the public, invariably applied to the only potentially worthwhile title offered – binding destroyed, lacking the odd illustration and exquisitely hand-coloured in juvenile wax crayon:
"That one has always been a favourite with the children."
Nicholas Willmott, Ipswich.

"Have much is this, please?"
It's free, Sir.
"Oh, that's all right, then. Here's three pence . . ."

"I've rebound two of them with cases taken from other books. Does that increase the value?"

"I like this series. I put them on the shelf above the desk, and the pages always fall out. There is no greater joy than putting them in the right order and sticking them back."

"I'd like to buy this book please."
Certainly . . . Oh, I'm sorry, but this is an odd volume. I don't want to split the set. I want to sell it with the others.
"Mmm. What if I was to buy two of the three?"

"These have been kept in the barn for a couple of years, but I expect they'll clean up. We brought a couple indoors for a day or two, and the smell very soon fades."
Nicholas Willmott, Ipswich.

"Excuse me. Did you give me that pound change?"
Yes, that's it there.
"Are you sure? You can't remember the number, can you?"
The Bookshop, Belfast.

"You've got a lot of books here, do you want some more?"

"I've travelled the country looking for this book. I've written to nearly every dealer in England and advertised in six different magazines and papers. I'd just about given up hope. How much is it?"
Two pounds, fifty pence.
"Oh, is that the best you can do?"
The Bookshop, Belfast.

"This one's got no price in it. Does that mean it's free?"
A. J. Redstone, Nottingham.

Do you have a price in mind, Sir?
"No, I haven't a clue. I'll leave it entirely to you."
How about a pound?
"One pound! I would have thought at least ten!"
Now we have a starting point.

"If I sell it, it will feel like I've lost a friend."
Room at the Top, Kingsbridge.

Customer viewing the section on sex:
"Oh, that's an interesting book on orgies. What a super book. Eighty pence! Oh, I don't think I could afford that!"
Old Soke Books, Peterborough.

Dear Mr. Jackson,
   I have received all three parcels, in good condition as well. Enclosed is a payment for the last parcel of books, except that I would like to bring up one point. When I consider the price of the book "A Report upon the Boreal Flora of the Sierra Nevada of California" by Frank Jason Smiley high, it is because of the condition of the book. You quoted the condition as a "Fine unopened copy in original wrappers." However, the problem with the book, is that none of the pages have been cut! Every page is joined to the next. Actually they are joined in sets of four pages . . . About 90% of the pages are not cut properly. I've spent a couple of hours carefully cutting down the edges between the pages using a sharp letter-opener. (Have got to page 200). However, the edges are somewhat ragged, especially the top seal which has a sort of perforation which leaves an especially ragged edge. The content of the book is most satisfactory and I would like to keep it, BUT is there any possibility that you would refund a portion of the $20 price? The $20 price seems excessive considering the condition of the book."
Ian Jackson, Berkeley, California.

"Sure you wouldn't pay that for it new!"
Customer handling a Wodehouse 1st edition at The Bookshop, Belfast.

"It would suit me better if we could work out a leasing arrangement . . ."
Louise McDermott, Rome, Italy.

"You don't buy desks, do you?"
Norman Lord, London.

"I have this book at home, will you buy it?"
What is it called?
"Oh, I can't remember, but it's [*measuring the air with her hands*] that big, that wide and has red covers. How much will you pay for it?"
William Dinner, Brighton.

"That's £2."
No, I'm ever so sorry, but it says £2.50.
"It says £2."
No, actually, it says £2.50, but I can get another opinion. Mike, is that £2 or £2.50?
It's £2.50.
"Well, it looks like £2 to me: that's the real price!"
But when the book was published it was £8.95!
"That's meaningless. My car was £7,000 originally but that's not its true value now."
He paid with great reluctance and drove off in his expensive car.

"But everyone else gives me ten percent!"
Gosford Books, Coventry.

I'm sorry, Sir, but I've just bought these and haven't priced them yet.
"Oh, not to worry, I've no money on me anyway."
The Bookshop, Belfast.

"How much do you pay for your books?"
What sort of books?
"Oh, you know, ones with pages."
Stephen Foster Books, Wandsworth.

"Can I buy a single book or do you only sell in bulk?"
Louise McDermott, Rome, Italy.

"I'll pay you £100 for the book but, could you please make the receipt out for £10 so my wife won't know how much I've spent!"
Famous Hollywood multi-millionaire, who also asked for the book to be delivered to The Savoy Hotel.
Norman Storey, London.

Elderly clergyman who wanted to squeeze every last penny from us:

"What about this one, then? What will you give me for it? I bet you're feeling out of your depth now! How much would you sell it for? I wonder what Blackwell's would offer me. I'll just give them a ring now to compare prices. That one is worth £100 you know. How much will you give me?"

I'm sorry, Sir, but I can't be rushed in this way. We deal in every subject under the sun, so we can't know everything, and we must work things out cautiously. We put our own money on the line, after all.

"I see. So, how much will you give me for that one? I'll let you have it for £95. £5 profit should be enough for you!"

"Why is there such a difference in price between paperbacks and leatherbound books? I buy paperbacks because they are cheaper!"

Room at the Top, Kingsbridge.

"Look, guv'nor, this book should interest you; my boy used it for science at school. True, it's been knocked about a bit, and a lot of pages are underlined in red ink, but it says FIRST EDITION inside, and that must make it a valuable book for you!"

Ben Kane Book Service, London.

"Do you buy books for cash or what?"

Vendors preferring to exchange for what could perhaps try Columbine Books, Southampton.

Finally, Nicholas Willmott of Ipswich relates the following dialogue between a vendor and a colleague of his:

"I wish to sell some books, they belonged to my son."

Oh, has he left home then?

"No, he was shot dead. But it's all right, only a few of the books got splashed."

GLUED · TO · A · BOOK . .

"I need another hundred paperbacks for my new bookcase but, this time could you stick them all together, otherwise my friends take them home to read?"
Mole Bookshop, East Molesey.

5 BOOKS BY THE YARD
(Or, The Mentality of Yuppiedom!)

"Can you do me six dozen books please?"
Certainly, what colour?
"I want two dozen black (perhaps with some black-and-white or grey); some really vivid greens, and some pinks. And can I have them by this afternoon?"

"You know, these little books are really cute! But back in the States, my customers, you know, they prefer the big books, and they think 'a big book, it's got to be a big price; a little book it's got to be a little price', so I can't afford to buy the little ones and ship 'em back to the States, but I think they're really cute."

"Oh, hello, ducks, I must tell you. At home I've got this sweet little carpenter and he's made me some really dinky shelving, and I'd like some books to fill them. Can you do me, in leather of course, about two feet of green, two feet of red and some bright blue?"

"If you get any books you want to throw away, just let us know, because we could do with some to fill our shelves. We've just had our lounge shelved in Georgian style, and it's lovely but we haven't got any books to put on them."

"I thought, maybe this could go with your other book."

"Oh, I've got some in leather . . ."

"Shall we have these?"
"Yeh, I think we ought'a. I just lurve brown."

"I don't know who this Fielding chap was, but they're sure cute bindings . . ."

"Have you got any books measuring about eight inches by five?"
Well, I dare say we could find some, but what sort of subject?
"Oh, anything, I'm not fussy. But I would like them to have nice covers."
Don't you even want particular authors, or illustrations, perhaps?
"No, I really don't care what the contents are so long as they look nice and are the right size."
Well, I'm sure we can find some, but, excuse my asking, what are you going to do with them?
"I'm going to remove the pages and put my videos in them. They'll look much better!"
Beck Head Books, Kirkby Lonsdale.

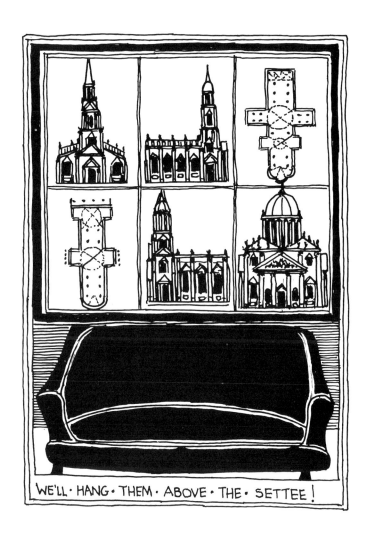

WE'LL · HANG · THEM · ABOVE · THE · SETTEE !

"Maybe we could mount them all in one frame to hang above the settee."
The book was the elephant folio *book called* Six Wren Churches.

"Well, I've always said that if someone was to buy a house and have a fitted bookshelf, this is the sort of place where he could come and buy them."
Note the singular 'shelf'.

"Ah just lurve books. Books are so pretty!"

"Hello, this is *XYZ* Furnishing here. We wondered if you would be interested in buying some books?"
Yes, of course, but what sort of books are they?
"They're the ones we've been using for display purposes in our shops."
I see. Does that mean you're not selling bookshelves any more?
"Not at all, but we've decided to use cardboard cut-out books from now on. The real books used to make the shelves sag so much . . ."
County Bookshop, Oakham.

"What do you do to make your books look old?"
Room at the Top, Kingsbridge.

"Look, I've got this great deal on. Can you sell me five thousand books, all hard back, in good condition, and they must measure exactly 7 inches by 3 by 1, and, err, I can't pay any more than forty pence each?"
Goodness, that's going to be difficult. I really don't think we'll be able to manage that. We just won't be able to find enough the right size at the right price, and it would take ages to organise. Can't you vary it a bit?
"No, the measurements are crucial."
Really? What on earth is this deal?
"Well, what we do, right, is, we bend them into *this* shape, opened out, because that's one of the most perfect shapes you can get. It's called the french curve. And then we dip them in this solution which makes them stiff and solid. We paint a bit of text on them, like 'Bless this House', bit of fancy lettering and decoration, you know the sort of thing. Then we dip them in a heavy gloss glaze and sell 'em as ornaments. They're paying me £1 a book and turning them round at £12 a time. If I can only find enough books I'll be all right, won't I?"

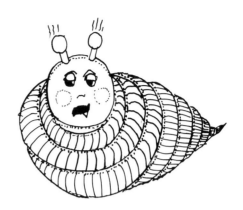

"... and we'll see what size books we'll need next. We might need some 10- or 11-inch ones."
Local large public school librarians.

"I prefer collecting stamps myself . . ."
Not a lot of reading in them, Sir.

"Livres, 35 francs per kilo."
Spotted by Stewart W. Gibb, Largs, at St. Nazaire, France. 'La Jeune Fille' at the 'Caisse' had a set of scales . . .

"I'd like this book please, it's half an inch thick."
I'm sorry?
"It's half an inch thick."
Aren't you going to read it?
"No! We've got an antique table at home but one leg's half an inch shorter than the others . . ."
David Johnstone, Eaton Ford.

"These aren't very pretty books, are they?"
Room at the Top, Kingsbridge.

"Here's a photograph of my son!"
Oh, that's nice! He's standing next to a collection of Heron Books! But what a pity he doesn't have any real books . . .
"Oh, you're right actually. How did you know it was just a pull-down blind?"
Chapel Collector's Centre, Castor.

"You know, maybe they're a bit small, but I suppose we could have them all put in one frame . . ."
This book was a volume containing thirty Japanese prints, each measuring about 8" by 12".

"I'd like to buy these books, but they're so grubby. Would you clean them for me first?"

Huge American wearing jeans and a large cowboy hat:
"Do you have this shop arranged at all?"
Yes, it is classified, what subject were you looking for?
"Well, how about by author?"
Yes, we have a fiction section and it's alphabetical; which writer were you looking for?
"Robert Louis Stevenson."
This way . . . Now, we have several titles, which one did you want?
[SILENCE]
Well, we have Travels With a Donkey, *and . . .*
"No, I'm looking for a little brown one . . ."
We don't have a little brown one; which title was it?
"It's called *Volume Seven*."
Err, what?
"Back in California, I bought a little brown set of Robert Louis Stevenson and Volume Seven is missing!"
Oh dear, what was it called?
"I don't know."

94

IT'S · CALLED · VOLUME · SEVEN ·....

"You mean you've *read* your modern first editions? You've actually *opened* them and turned the pages? I wouldn't dream of buying them from you – I'm a serious collector!"
Graham Hodge, Wellingborough.

"The nice thing about large old books is that they always make a room look cosy . . ."

"Can you do me a quantity of hardbacks at 10p each?"
Yes, certainly. How many would you like?
"Oh, I don't mind, but they've got to be good condition, perhaps dust wrappers . . ."
Right, it won't take me long . . .
There you are: 65 books at 10p each, that's £6.50 please. Of course, if you were prepared to pay more per book, we could supply a much better quality selection.
"What sort of figures are we talking of?"
Well, we could do a lot at 25p each, but at 50p we would even colour-co-ordinate them for you.
"How many could you do at 25p each?"
How about 100?
"All right, I'll be back in twenty minutes."
I gathered 100 awful books from our backstock: maths textbooks from the 1930s, out-of-date technical books, the Bible, Tennyson, a few novels we had hundreds of copies of. The customer returned and we put the books in his car without checking them, and he paid me £25 in notes. Then I asked 'What are you going to use them for?' I expected him to reply that he had a deal to supply a show house or something like that, but he said:
"Oh, just reading material. You haven't found anything for me for so long. I can always give them away to Oxfam when I've finished."

The same customer returned a few days later and the following dialogue took place:
Hello, how are you?
"Very well, thank you."
Been doing much reading lately?
"Oh yes, and some sorting out too. Have you any AA books? . . . Right, can I give you a pound for those?"
Pardon?
"Well, you said at fifty pence each I could have anything."

"I'm looking for something this high, this wide and white . . ."
Oban Antiques, Oban.

"Oh no! They must be in English because we always read them. We use them as reference for the children. We always buy them to read you know. We just prefer the old leather-bound volumes . . ."

"Why do you put them on shelves?"
Room at the Top, Kingsbridge.

"Now, colours! Mmm, what sort of colours are the books you haven't got?"

"Are you going to specialise in anything in your new shop?"
Well, actually, we were thinking of stocking only green books.
"Oh, they won't sell!"
I'm sorry?
"No, it's true. When I worked for W.H. Smith we were taught not to stock green books because they didn't sell. Now, yellow, that's a good selling colour!"

"I tell you what, as you're selling me over a thousand books for the library, you can put your bookplate in each one if you like, as an advertisement."
Sir, considering the quality of books you're going to buy, I think you can put your own bookplate in.

The same man interviewed in The Observer's *'Room of my Own' commented in his bookless lounge:*
"The books on the table below belong to Wendy and are not books at all but a miniature bar concealing a set of bottles."

"I want a copy of *Our Mutual Friend* . . .
No, my daughter wants one in paperback. She thinks it suits the modern decor of her bedroom more . . ."

There was another deal, to supply 1000 hardbacks at 50p each, to be used as furniture for showhouses:
Do you want dustwrappers on them?
"No, that doesn't really matter because we're going to take most of them off, so that we can colour-co-ordinate."

"I think these should match the curtains behind the wall unit."
SPCA Charity Bookshop, Malta.

"So, why are there three plates missing?"
Well, I suppose a previous owner of the book liked them so much that he took them out and framed them. It does happen . . .
"Oh! But that doesn't do the book any good, does it?"
I suppose not, Sir.
Ken Spelman's, York.

"Oh, these should look nice on the shelf!"

"Dear Sirs,
We are fitting out a client's flat in Monte Carlo with oak panelling and fitted bookshelves. Our client has intimated that he would like old leather-bound books to fill the shelves. Can you supply? The approximate area we wish to cover will be forty square metres."
It was hard work, but eventually we managed to supply two thousand leather bindings at £4 each.

"That book you bought the other day – I want it back. My assistant wasn't supposed to sell it because it's part of the fixtures of the shop. It was screwed to the wall after all."

"I wonder, do you have any Hayne's Car Manuals? I want as many as possible – I'm making a statue out of them and I've nearly finished!"

FABLON........

"I have to cover all my books in matching fablon – it's the only way my wife will let them into the house!"
Robert Vaughan, Stratford-upon-Avon.
Think about it! Which should we feel most pity for? The husband, the wife, or the books?

THANK · YOU · FOR · RECOMMENDING · THAT · BOOK

Lady holding very small poodle:
"Have you got any books on how to press flowers: which ones to choose and what time of year to do it, that sort of thing?"
No, but we've got a super book on taxidermy.
"Haw, haw, it's almost the same thing . . ."

100

6 GETTING EVEN

"Have you got any books on shooting things?"
Animals or people, Madam?
"Well, animals of course."
Sue, could you show the lady where the books on killing animals are?
"Well, not necessarily killing!"
Sue, could you show the lady where the books on maiming animals are?

"Oh, you've got books here!"
Yes, Madam, we're a bookshop.
Books Etc., Stamford.

"Are you open tomorrow morning, about 12 o'clock?"
Yes, we're always open at that time.
"Oh, good. Only, you see, a *Government Minister* will be visiting you tomorrow, and you wouldn't like him to be standing outside on the pavement, unable to get in, *would you?*"
No, I suppose not. We wouldn't like any customer to be standing outside, unable to get in.
"Eeeugh."
(I'm not sure how to spell the noise which means "Oh', but slightly offended, in a grating public-school accent'. It's such a strange, animal sound.)

Anyway, this very important Government Minister, with a special interest in education, commented:
"Oh! You've got a copy of Duff's *Handbook on Hanging*. That's a very rare book. I've got a copy myself, actually."
This was not the end of the matter, for his wife picked up a copy of The Directory of Ladies of Pleasure in Edinburgh *(a reprint of an eighteenth-century work) and announced:*
"Oh! I'm from Edinburgh!"

"I can't get this book back on the shelf!"
That's right, we have an automatic shelf-closing system here. Once you've removed a book, we'd rather you took it away.

"Look, err, I'm in the trade. I'm in publishing. Do you think you could possibly . . . ease the price for me?"
Well, I'll see what I can do. [the book turned out to be a 30p paperback]. Well, I can't really give you any discount on 30p, but you can have the book with my compliments if it means so much to you.
"Oh, thank you very much."
He started to shuffle out, feeling a little embarrassed, when another customer, a regular, pitched in:
"Give him ten pence from me from out of the till, will you, Mike, so he can get himself a cup of tea?"

HERE'S · 10 P. · FOR · A · CUP · OF · TEA!

What sort of books do you like?
"Oh, anything."
I don't believe you!
"Oh, yes, anything."
Right then, how about a copy of The Sociology of Nigerian Education?
"No."
Oh, well, how about The Brass Industry in Uttar Pradesh?
"Err, I see what you mean."
He left twenty minutes later without buying. I was right!

103

"I'm looking for stone hot-water bottles for my wife's collection . . ."
Mmm, perhaps I could sell you a new brain . . .
Blitzgeist Bookshop, Birmingham.

"Well, the thing is, we weren't expecting you in today, and your books were too valuable to leave in the shop overnight . . ."
Playing for time at The Bookshop, Belfast, after having accidentally thrown some useless books on the skip. They were later retrieved after much digging at the tip. [When we take books to the tip they usually come back to us a day later anyway.]

"How much is that, please?"
Ah! that's £110, Sir.
"Really? I had a better one than that, and I threw it on the tip!"
Are you on a coach-trip?
"Err, yes, but why do you ask?"
If you hadn't thrown it away you might have been able to afford a car.
Oban Antiques, Oban.

Wife of local Conservative Big Name:
"I have three books on cookery here. Which one do you think I should buy?"
Madam, I cannot make the decision for you. You have to take responsibility for your own life in your own hands. We're not running a nanny state, you know.
She liked the answer so much she bought all three!

"Yes, very nice, but I don't see how they would fit into the reading scheme."
Headmaster of local impoverished primary school, on being offered a gift of boxes of lovely, brand-new but slightly soiled children's books for his badly-stocked school library. Who can help us if we can't even give them away?

May I perform a cashectomy on you, Sir?

"I'll take it now and pay you next week. Honest, I'm a man of my word."
Yes, it's always the self-knowledge which is the most difficult to attain.

"Where's that book I saw last week?"
I've sold it, Sir. It's always the books that you don't buy that you regret, isn't it?

"Shaun, is it still quiet today?"
Yes, I'm afraid so.
"Right, take all the antiquarian books out of the window and fill it with Mills and Boon."
What?
"Do as you're told. Let's give 'em what they want. We've had enough of this 'pearls before swine' nonsense."
All right then.
I hadn't even finished filling the window when a customer walked in:
"How much are your Mills and Boon? I'll take the lot!"
And so he did! The Boss was right!

"Thirty pence! Is that all the Word of God is worth?"
Well, maybe it's priced so cheaply in order to allow poorer people to buy it.
"Oh, I see! What a lovely thought."
I only said maybe.

"I've come in here so I can let my children free at last. Now I can relax! It was such an effort hanging on to them in the antique shop!"
Beck Head Books, Kirkby Lonsdale.

"I think it's *terrible*, you dealers tearing up books to take the pictures out. Really disgusting!"
But, please, we would never *do it unless there was a profit in it!*

"If you were to put the books in my safe, I might then lend you the money to buy them."
The bank manager of one of our colleagues.

The bank manager of another colleague advised the following:
"Look, in my experience of dealing with second-hand bookshops, I find that they cannot survive without also selling a bit of pornography on the side, so I strongly recommend that you also get into that line."

"No point in asking in here because I asked last week."

"You're not closing for lunch, are you?"
It doesn't look like it . . .

I'm sorry, Sir, but without a title or an author I'm going to have difficulty finding it.

"Will you take a fiver for this?"
If that's all you think it's worth . . .

"No, we might pay £6 for a book, but we're not paying it for a scrap of paper."
The response from the Isle of Wight Record Office when we offered them a collection of original medieval charters relating to the island. If they'd said 'Thank you very much but we can't afford them', we would at least have sent them some free photocopies, as we did for other record offices!

106

NO; DO · WHAT · YOU · LIKE . . . .

On a very hot humid day the following incident occurred:
A middle-aged lady dressed in tweeds with a sort of 'school-mistress' appearance marched into the shop and barked aggressively:
"PROHIBITION?"
No, you can do whatever you like in here!
Oh, I'm sorry if you don't find that funny, it's a very hot day.
"No, I don't!"
Shaun, I think we've lost a customer.

107

"Excuse me, I can understand this one being £1.50 when it was published at £3; but why is this paperback £1 when it was first published at 2/6d?"
Madam, if you are stupid enough to ask the question, you're not going to understand the answer.
(I thought it best to leave the name of this dealer out.)

Aggressive American lady throwing a book on the table:
"That isn't worth half what you have on it!"
Really, Madam? In that case why not have half the book? (tearing it in two)
Nial Devitt Books, Leamington Spa.

"Do you have Herodotus?"
I used to have, Sir, but I've been cured.

Hey, that's a nice item. You know who will buy that?
"Yes. Stick £12 on it. He'll *have* to have it, won't he?"

"But you can't be a bookdealer – you're a woman!"
Room at the Top, Kingsbridge.

"I cannot see what people see in books."
It's black maggots on white snow, Madam.
Blitzgeist Bookshop, Birmingham.

"But why is it so expensive?"
Well, Sir, if you would like to sell us your house at its 1953 price, you could have the book with our compliments . . .

"So, you're not giving anything away, then!"
No. In theory we're in business to sell books, Sir.

After offering realistic prices for individual books and being turned down so often because the customer didn't realise they were worth so much, we adopted the tactic of working-out a fair price for the lot, but emphasising the importance of a particular duff book. In rich households this would invariably produce the response:
"Yes, OK, fair enough; but I think I'll keep that particular one. You can buy the rest."

Hello, Sir! We've got a copy of your new book in. Would you like to sign it for us?
"Yes, of course . . . That will be fifty pence, please."

"There's a book . . ."
Look no further, Sir! We have it! Here you are: Oscar Smart's The Inheritance of Fecundity in Fowles.
"Err, no, it wasn't that one . . ."
What a pity . . .

"I expect you remember me!"
No, Sir. Who are you?

"Are your books in any kind of order?"
Well, they used to be, but we found that the larger books didn't fit the shelves, so we just gave up.
Rutland Bookshop, Uppingham.

"I must come again when I've got more time."
Madam, if you cannot see anything in this shop which excites, stimulates and prompts you to buy, you're probably either officially brain-dead or a brummy.
The Blitzgeist Bookshop, Birmingham.

"I could never do your job. I just couldn't stand the boredom!"

"I suppose you really want them sectionalised, don't you? Still, I suppose you're not really bothered."

"Ah! I see you've got a copy of Cole's *Antiquarian and Secondhand Bookdealers Active in Britain*. That won't include you, then."

"Here's a book about Systems Analysis – something you've never studied!"

"Shaun, I really think you would make more impact as a manager if you didn't keep making that silly little laugh every time you stop talking."

"Shaun's quite a sweet, furry creature, isn't he? Rather like one of those things on *Fraggle Rock*. If you came to visit us, my Mum would give you an enormous piece of cake with cream on top. But then, I don't suppose my Dad would let you in."

"Shaun, your whole attitude to literature is lacking in sensitivity, good taste and refinement!"

A note pushed through the letter-box:
"I have come from Halifax to look at your books but find you closed. I would have been wasting my time as I can see through your window that you only stock ten-pence books."
Border Bookshop, Todmorden.

"Come to Old Constable's Bookshop for a gob-full of culture!"
A rejected advertisement which we had wanted to place in a local arts publication. They pretended that there was no space until we offered to change the wording!

HEALTH · FARM · FOR · TORTOISES

"Honestly, it's like a health farm for tortoises in here!"

"Does your dog bite?"
Yes, he's a spray-painted pit bull.
The Observatory, Sitka, Alaska.

The most irritating aspect of offering free coffee to customers is the difficulty of getting a straight answer out of them. They say thank you for offering but don't say yes or no. They say yes, but won't answer how they want it. Or they give you the wrong instructions but expect you to understand that 'as it comes' cannot possibly mean 'white with sugar'. They ask all their friends before answering for themselves, or offer it to their friends as if it had been arranged by them. Sometimes they demand the coffee from you as if they were paying for it, clicking their fingers in the air as they do so, and sometimes they refuse the coffee but demand something else instead. But the majority appreciate it, and we are still convinced it's the right thing to do. And it provides another opportunity for dialogue with the customers:

Would you like some coffee? We've just made some.
"No, it's disgusting stuff. Don't you know it caused the downfall of the British Empire?"

"Why have you offered coffee to everyone else but not to me? Mind you remember next time."

Would you like a cup of coffee?
"Oh, yes please. White with lots of sugar."
Here you are . . .
"Oh God! Call that a helping? I could do with six of them!"

"Not big spenders today, thank you very much. Still, we haven't drunk you out of coffee either."
Customers to whom I hadn't got round to offering coffee.

Do you like the coffee this morning?
"Yes, it's delicious. Why, is there something wrong with it?"
Sort of, I thought I'd try decaffeinated today.
"Well, that's not going to do me any good!"
Dialogue with the Boss . . .

We once had a window-display full of books and prints about foxhunting. We couldn't resist placing a notice with them saying 'An exciting display, graphically illustrating the premature deaths of defenceless animals'. Later on a man came up to the boss in the street and said 'I'd just like to congratulate you on that marvellous display last week. I think it's first rate that people like you stand up for what you believe in. Well done!' *To which the boss replied:* 'Oh, hold your praise for the moment, we're doing another one!'
'Oh, marvellous, what's that?'
'We're going to have a window-full of books on freemasonry. We have a special collection on its way here now. My assistant and I will be wearing little leather aprons all week, and, of course, if anyone buys a book, we'll say 'thank you very much' in the customary way.' *With bizarre gesture.*
A few days later he was advised formally that he would never be invited to be a mason.

A collector friend of the Blitzgeist Bookshop, Birmingham is extremely knowledgeable about Japanese and German rare books. They recently visited a book fair together, and while they were examining a particularly choice item the woman bookdealer acidly remarked:
"You'll find no pictures in it, you know!"
Neither the friend nor the Blitzgeist people suffer fools gladly, so he replied:
"That's a shame, because I've brought along my f....... coloured pencils!"

We were asked to advertise for a copy of Debrett's Peerage *by a lady member of the local aristocracy. We advertised four or five times before we located one, and then we offered it to the lady at £5. On the telephone she exclaimed:*
"FIVE POUNDS! I'm not going to pay you five pounds for that! You can stick it on your shelf and wait for it to sell, and when nobody's bought it in six months' time, I shall come and pay you £2.50 for it. Goodbye!"
We priced the book at £8 and it sold within a week.

Would you like a bag for it, hang the expense?

"Do you have a theology section? My father's a priest, actually, so he could come in and make some sort of judgement."
Do priests usually make judgements?

"Eee, we've got so many books at home, we could open up our own shop!"
Really, how many have you got?
"Oh, it must be at least five hundred."

"Where do you keep Dickens?"
He's dead, Sir.
"Yes, I know that, but where is he?"
I don't know. I suppose it might be worthwhile trying Westminster Abbey.

"I only collect books with peacock designs on the endpapers. Do you have any?"
No, we don't, Sir. Try us again when you have wider interests.

"Does one send an account?"
No, Madam, one pays.

ENCOUNTERS WITH SOME OTHER DEALERS:
(Names avoided to spare the guilty!)

"Oh, thank goodness you're open. I've been trying to get into this shop for two years."
I'm sorry, but we're closed.
"But the sign on the door says 'Open'!"
Not on this side it doesn't.
Related by a colleague.

Dealer buying very large quantity of sport books:
"You've got quite a comprehensive sport section . . ."
Yes, we like it as a subject, it always sells well. The only ones we don't particularly like to stock are books on 'field sports'.
"Oh, you're one of those, are you?"
I don't care for hunting, no.
"Well, you'd better not tell my wife that or the whole deal will be off."

Dealer whom we had rung about his unpaid bill:
"Normally I'm far too busy to chase my own unpaid invoices. You can't be doing much business."

"If you are a browser, wipe your feet when you come in."

"Don't touch the books!"

"Most reasonably priced books are on the floor."
Astounding notice lying on top of floor-pile.

"Books are beautiful!"
Inane poster at local evangelical bookshop.

"Have you got anything on fungi?"
I don't know, who wrote it?
[One of our customers at a very large, well-known new bookshop in London.]

"Hello, may I just look round?"
No.
"But I might buy a book!"
I don't want you to buy a book. I want you to go away.
Anonymous dealer, narrated by a colleague.

"Would you leave your bag with us; we have had things stolen in the past . . ."

"Ah, now I can see that you're a young man in a hurry, so sit yourself down and relax. You and me, we're going to talk about books. But first, have you heard the cricket scores?"
The boss finally left three hours later having been refused permission to buy a single book!

"Hello, I hope you don't mind me asking, but any chance of any trade discount on something so minuscule? They come to £12 the pair."
I can't imagine a gentler way of asking this question, but she looked me up and down in the most offensive manner and said:
"No, I don't think so."
My experience in a Cambridge bookshop. What a strange accent they speak in that place.

"The total comes to £103. Now, 10% trade discount . . . Round it down to £100."

"Well, I've got to hand it to you, you do have an eye for a tatty book."

"We no longer bother putting the opening times on the door –
then it doesn't matter if we're not here!"

"What are you talking about? You're so enthusiastic! I became a
bookdealer to give up work, not to start it!"

"No, I don't think we can serve you at the moment, we're doing a stock-take."
It's both sad and naive to make the bureaucracy more important than the business!

Dealer selling a book to one of our customers:
"Book-collecting is a disease and I'm a very expensive doctor."
Doesn't anyone offer a cure?

"No, I couldn't buy those – more than my job's worth!"
Some dealers can be incredibly dismissive when buying books.

"Hello, it's Shaun Tyas from Goldmark Books. You may remember having sold me a few items through the post?"
Yes, that's right. What can I do for you?
"Well, I'll be in the area tomorrow, and I wondered if I could call on you and perhaps buy something else?"
Certainly! See you in the afternoon?
"Yes, that's fine, and there'll be my brother and a friend with me, too."
Oh no. Only one at a time.
"But I can't leave them in the car. They're book-lovers too!"
Well, I'll not make an exception.
"Well, I'm sorry but that means I can't come at all."
Fair enough. Goodbye.

"That comes to £342 and fifteen pence. Tell you what, forget the fifteen pence."

"If you're not going to buy a book, then get out of my shop!"

"It's the dirty shoes I'm looking at. Do you mind not coming in when it's raining?"

"The back of your shirt is rather dirty."

"Hello, is Martin there please?"
No I'm afraid not, can I help you?
"Oh, possibly, I wanted to sell him a book. It's a nice copy of Baines' *History of the Wars of the French Revolution*."
Oh, sounds all right. Why do you want to offer it to Martin instead of to me?
"Oh, I'm sorry, but I've always assumed that Martin was the proprietor."
Listen, I'm sick of people thinking Martin's the proprietor! For your information I happen to be the poor sod who runs this bloody business. Goodbye!

I related this incident to a customer and he immediately picked up the telephone and rang this dealer himself:
"Hello, Mr. P . . .? I wonder, do you have a copy of Edward Baines' early book on the Napoleonic Wars? I'm desperate for a copy."
There's nobody here who can help you today. I only answered the telephone because I thought it might be my wife with some important news. I'm doing a very important marketing exercise at the moment. I've got publishers and other dealers here and I can't be bothered with trivialities. You'll have to try again some other day.
And down went the telephone. I wonder what advice the assembled experts gave him!

Remember to close the door when you leave.

AN ADVANCE COMMENT ON THIS BOOK
FROM A LOCAL DEALER WHOSE NAME HAS NOW
BEEN OMITTED!

"No, I didn't like it, Shaun. Some of the anecdotes were very amusing, and it was certainly a good idea, but it got rather repetitive and, to be blunt, boring. Now, the cartoons I thought were absolutely superb, they were the real making of the book. The Introduction I didn't like at all. It was a long-winded, boring, pompous winge against customers, and a puff on Goldmark's. Frankly, given the nature of the book, I don't think I want our name associated with it!"

PUBLISHERS

"Before you go any further, I can tell you now that we're just not interested."

"No, we're not accepting *any* unsolicited material until 1990!"

"No, not really the sort of thing which a large commercial concern like ourselves would want to bother with."

EXTRA QUOTES

Martin Smith in Heffer's bookshop,
Cambridge:

"Have you got a copy of the <u>Glastonbury</u>
<u>Festival Handbook?</u>"

We don't stock <u>that sort of thing</u> here, Sir

BOOKWORM DROPPINGS